T0077920

The Heart of
BETHLEHEM

A Twenty-Five Day Journey of Faith for the Christmas Season

Carol B. Weaver

WESTBOW
PRESS®
A DIVISION OF THOMAS NELSON
& ZONDERVAN

Scriptures taken from the Holy Bible, New International Version®, NIV®. Copyright © 1973, 1978, 1984, 2011 by Biblica, Inc.™ Used by permission of Zondervan. All rights reserved worldwide. www.zondervan.com The "NIV" and "New International Version" are trademarks registered in the United States Patent and Trademark Office by Biblica, Inc.™

Scripture quotations are taken from the Holy Bible, New Living Translation, copyright ©1996, 2004, 2007, 2013, 2015 by Tyndale House Foundation. Used by permission of Tyndale House Publishers, Inc., Carol Stream, Illinois 60188. All rights reserved.

"Scripture quotations are from the ESV® Bible (The Holy Bible, English Standard Version®), copyright © 2001 by Crossway, a publishing ministry of Good News Publishers. Used by permission. All rights reserved."

WestBow Press books may be ordered through booksellers or by contacting:

WestBow Press
A Division of Thomas Nelson & Zondervan
1663 Liberty Drive
Bloomington, IN 47403
www.westbowpress.com
1 (866) 928-1240

ISBN: 978-1-9736-0782-3 (sc)
ISBN: 978-1-9736-0781-6 (e)

Print information available on the last page.

WestBow Press rev. date: 11/01/2017

To my mom.
Without her, my children would not have an
Advent box or a mom who loves Jesus.

Contents

Preface

It all began with an Advent box and a desire to instill the truth of God's Word into my three small children. The box, a gift from my mom. It was through her illness and death that I began my journey of faith. A journey I never expected to include writing a book.

From a bed in ICU, my mom witnessed to me for the first time revealing her trust in Jesus. It was then and there He captured my heart through the comfort He provided my mom. My pursuit of Him led to searching out the Christmas story in its entirety and dividing it into twenty-five sections. I added labels inside the door of each small cubby of the Advent box with the Bible verses to read while my children enjoyed whatever small treat fit in the box.

As the years went by and my children grew, my faith and desire for others to know the truth also grew. A phone call from a high school friend I hadn't spoken to in years opened my heart to the reality of where most people stand with the Truth. In the catching up conversation, I shared how God kept me busy teaching Sunday School, leading Bible studies and prayer groups. Her response... *I used to do the church thing, but I don't anymore...* broke my heart. I realized she didn't get it. She saw church as an institution and not as a relationship with your Savior. She saw church as a way to fill time, not build faith.

That conversation led me to study the Nativity story, looking for truth, asking questions, seeking answers with my family as we approached Christmas each December. The questions and answers, over the years, became devotionals. The devotionals became a booklet, the booklet a Christmas card sent out to friends and family, with my dear friend from high school in mind.

After several rewrites and rejections, you have before you the results of a journey of faith. One I hope you will share with your family and friends, finding faith and not just filling time, as you approach Christmas year after year.

Acknowledgements

First and foremost, I thank God — Father, Son, Spirit — without whom I can do nothing (John 15:5). He alone provided the catalyst, inspiration, faith, courage, and opportunities to begin seeking, writing, and publishing.

Secondly, to Stacy Boyer and her encouragement to use a gift I thought long buried and beyond revival.

Next, sisters in faith: my cousin Mary Lynn Smith, my sister-in-law Ginger Boone, my sister Betsy Luzader, and my dear friend Sarah Hugghins. Each graciously received, read, edited, critiqued, and encouraged the writing of these devotionals somewhere along the way.

I thank God for my children — Rachel, Luke, and Morgan — and their willingness to sit and listen to God's Word, ask questions, participate and endure, even on days when we were running late for school. Thankful that each has grown into a believing soul in spite of their mother.

Finally, thanks to my husband, Craig, a work of faith in progress, whom God uses to affirm His call with his agreement. I love you.

Introduction

The Heart of Bethlehem

For to us a child is born, to us a son is given…
Isaiah 9:6

No one strives to be ordinary. The Creator of the human heart instills into each soul the desire for a unique and meaningful life. Money, fame, power, or the perfect relationship appears on the world's horizon as a glimmering oasis — an escape from insignificance. But, just like a mirage, the world's way never satisfies. Only the One who knows our hearts holds the secret for transforming the ordinary into the extraordinary: Jesus Christ, the Son of God.

At the heart of Bethlehem lies the supernatural power of God breaking through the mundane and making it remarkable…

…a feed trough in Bethlehem, a crib for a King…

…a baby boy, God among us…

…a star in the sky, a beacon for wise men to follow… God began a story in Bethlehem He longs to continue in the heart of every person ever created. The birth of His Son into the lives of those He loves, transforming the ordinary into the extraordinary, through faith and trust.

God's trust is that He gives me Himself as a babe.
God expects my personal life to be a "Bethlehem." –
Oswald Chambers, *My Utmost for His Highest*

When we receive Jesus as Savior, we welcome Him as a *babe* — our hearts a Bethlehem. Jesus didn't stay an infant... He grew to be a man. A man who performed miracles, walked on water, and defeated death. God trusts us as spiritual newborns to give His Son room to grow. The more space we give Him — obeying His Word and choosing His will over our own — the more amazing our lives become.

Nothing compares to the experience of pursuing a relationship with your Creator. My relationship with Him has been quite a journey. God awakened desires and gifts I thought long dead. Walking with Him by faith leads to redemption and joy in unexpected places.

I pray your journey through *The Heart of Bethlehem* will spark a desire to embrace the hope found in Christ — *to us a child is born.* God's transforming love was never more evident or glorious than through the life of His Son, Jesus.

May the Holy Spirit prepare you to fully
receive and nurture the Babe in the
manger, and may He grow to reveal God's
glorious love in and through your life.

Merry Christmas, from an ordinary Christian,

Carol B. Weaver

Guidelines for the Journey

Blessed are those whose strength is in you,
whose hearts are set on pilgrimage.
Psalm 84:5

Start each day's journey of faith with prayer. The daily readings begin with a short Scripture-based prayer to help you get started (the Scripture reference is in parentheses). Ask God to be with you as you read His Word and show you what He wants you to know.

Read the verses for the day from your Bible. Scriptures used are from the New International Version Bible (NIV), unless otherwise noted. Translations vary in the exact wording, however the basic meaning is the same.

Read the day's writing and consider the questions. The questions are designed to help you think about what you have read and challenge you to consider how God's Word might affect your life.

Close in prayer. Ask God to reveal the truth of His Word to you. Ask how He wants you to respond. Test everything you are taught about God's Word with prayerful discernment. Through the Holy Spirit, God will confirm or correct the teaching.

Journal. Take time to write down insights you've gained or questions you have about what you have read. This practice helps you to remember your initial impressions. The more you remember what God has impressed on you, the more likely you are to continue to seek Him.

Heavenly, Father, unfold the meaning of Your words and give me "light." I confess, I am in the dark when it comes to Your Word — I need Your understanding. (Psalm 119:130)

December 1
24 Days til Christmas

Compelled to Tell

Luke 1:1-4

My mom lay in ICU battling pulmonary fibrosis, a lung disease that literally takes your breath away. With my three-month old on my lap, I sat in the waiting room. My older brother joined me after praying with her. He shared her words: *I trust, I trust.* In an instant, my heart was no longer my own. The revelation of knowing *my mom* trusted Jesus with her life launched me on a personal journey to seek out the reality of Christ for myself.

Luke didn't know Jesus personally, but he knew those who had. Inspired by those relationships, he set out to thoroughly investigate the life and ministry of Jesus for himself. Along the way, he became a passionate Believer. In order to encourage a friend in the faith, he shared his detailed account of Jesus's life, which we know as the New Testament book Luke.

My personal investigation began with prayer and the Bible — I knew of no other resources available to acquaint myself with the One who stole my heart. The more time I spent seeking Him, the more I recognized His presence in my life. I couldn't keep Him to myself. My children were the first to hear my revelations. I wanted them to know His love and grow to trust Him more than I ever had.

Just as Luke's letter to his friend produced a ripple effect — reaching others in an ever-widening circle — so did the audience with whom I shared my experiences. Family... friends... Sunday school... Bible studies... each subjected to my need to tell what I discovered. I went so far as to write and send a twenty-five day devotional as my Christmas card one year — the beginnings of what you are now reading. When the truth about Jesus impacts your life and becomes reality, you can't *not* share it.

Knowing and accepting or rejecting the truth about Jesus has eternal consequences. Luke's Spirit-inspired account of Jesus's life has endured and encouraged belief for more than a thousand years. Many strive to discount God and deny the reality of His Son. A denial made more difficult by the meticulous details of Luke's gospel. Archeologists continue to dig up evidence confirming the credibility of the gospels, details that help remove doubt.[1] But the best evidence for Jesus is not historical. It's the transformed lives of those who come close to Him. Those who tell what they know and live a life of faith.

---

1 *The Case for Christ* by Lee Strobel is a great book for anyone who wants to know more about the physical evidence for Jesus's life on earth.

Have you ever doubted that Jesus was a real man with a documented history?

When was the last time you were compelled to share the truth of Jesus with someone you love?

Heavenly Father, help me to know the reality of Jesus.

Lord, help me understand Your teaching, so I can recognize Your wonders. (Psalm 119:27)

December 2
23 Days til Christmas

Beyond Imagination

John 1:1-5, 14

John — gospel writer, disciple, beloved friend of Jesus — introduces Jesus as *the Word*. A name of significance for the two primary cultures who first read John's gospel: the Jews and the Greeks.

In Hebrew, *the Word* was used as a traditional reference to God. For Greeks, the term *word*, when applied universally, represented "the rational principle that governs all things."[2] John didn't want his audience to miss the truth — Jesus is God — the Principle who rules all things. A truth worth contemplating.

God — the one and only God, a unique individual Being, consisting in three persons: Father, Son, and Holy Spirit — entered the world of His creation as a baby. The God of the universe, all powerful, infinite in magnitude and glory — *uncontainable* — placed Himself in the care

---

2 New International Version Study Bible 1984 note, John 1:1

of a teenage mother and a poor carpenter. He stooped down to a position devoid of power, honor, and grandeur...

> *He had no beauty or majesty to attract us to him, nothing in his appearance that we should desire him.* — Isaiah 53:2

He came to reveal His Father's heart to a rebellious world and rescue the ones He loves — people whom He created for His glory and their joy through personal relationship.

God took a great risk creating mankind. True love only exists between individuals with free-will. He knew any form of rebellion against Himself — the Holy Creator — would destroy the possibility of relationship. Adam and Eve, within just a few short verses of creation, exercised their free-will making themselves the parents of a long line of rebels. God knows we are lost apart from Him. Moved by His great love and mercy, He sent His Son to make a way for us to return to Him and be forgiven.

God's Law came through His chosen people, the Israelites, and clearly laid out the price for forgiveness: the shedding of blood (Leviticus 17:11). As established with Passover during the Exodus, the blood of a perfect lamb or young goat temporarily provided forgiveness for a family's sin. On the cross, all the sins of the world — past, present, and future — were placed on Jesus. His blood paid the price for our sins perfectly and completely. Jesus, God in human form — sinless — came to be *the Lamb of God, who takes away the sin of the world!* (John 1:29).

Christianity is the sole religion with a God so defined by love He *willingly* sacrificed Himself for the redemption of His creation. No other religion proclaims a god who pays the penalty for their creatures' rebellion. Human imagination could never conjure up the truth: the God of the universe *chose* to become a man — the Uncontainable contained in fragile human form — to suffer and die at the hand of His creation, for the sake of His creation. Jesus was that man. *The Word made flesh.*

Have you ever considered Jesus as God in human form? What does that tell you about His character?

How does the uniqueness of the God of Christianity among all world religions influence your view of Christianity?

Lord, help me to understand the mystery of an infinite God with the power and desire to limit Himself to a finite human body for the sake of His creation.

Father God, light my path, bless me with understanding and insight regarding Your Word. (Psalm 119:105)

December 3
22 Days til Christmas

Undistractable

Luke 1:5-7

Judea: the nation of Jerusalem, home of the temple, a land of promise forfeited by sin. Hundreds of years had passed since the Israelites enjoyed a united faith and the full blessings of the Promised Land. The fall of their forefathers to the cultural temptations of the world brought them to "the time of Herod king of Judea" — a brutal ruler under the authority of Rome trying to keep peace in a country characterized by cultural diversity.

Hostile races and religions defiled the Holy Land. Sin brought corruption to the Jewish nation and to their religion. Judaism reflected the surrounding culture — opposing sects, splintered and fragmented — the temple a religious battleground.

In the midst of these cultural and religious distractions lived Zechariah and Elizabeth, "upright in the sight of God." Both had family roots reaching back to Aaron, the original High Priest. This devout couple resisted the temptation of assimilation — moving against the grain of their forefathers — they remained undistractable in the face of cultural chaos.

External distractions weren't the only pressures testing the faith of Zechariah and Elizabeth; they also wrestled with the personal disappointment of being childless. Ancient Jewish culture considered it a curse to be barren — a sign of God's disapproval. Just imagine this couple's life...

> ...their quiet home a daily reminder of their personal heartbreak...

> ...neighbors who assumed they were cursed by God...

> ...the temptation and availability of other gods with promises of fertility...

Emotional, spiritual, and physical reasons for rejecting their faith, yet Zechariah and Elizabeth continued to follow and serve God.

The world we live in today doesn't sound much different. A culture filled with distractions and oppositions to Christianity. Our "one nation under God" is moving farther and farther from Him. Other faiths making their way into the mainstream include Islam, Scientology, New Age spirituality, and atheism. Extensive division exists in the Christian community: Baptist, Catholic, Methodist, Presbyterian, and on and on. People facing infertility, chronic illness, or loneliness wonder if they have been rejected by God. The world makes available numerous alternatives to faith in the Gospel. Given the right circumstances, they seem reasonable and offer clear justification for rejecting God and His way. However, the ultimate question is: *Do you trust God?*

Faith is based on trust. Do you trust God to be who He says He is? Do you believe He is good, all-powerful, and loving? Do you trust Him to know what is best for you? Do you trust ~~that~~ He has a plan and purpose for your life? For thousands of years, God's followers have faced distractions and temptations from the world around them. Today's world is no exception. Follow the example of Zechariah and Elizabeth. Be *undistractable*. Faithfully trust God, in spite of your circumstances.

> *And without faith it is impossible to please God, because anyone who comes to him must believe that he exists and that he rewards those who earnestly seek him.* — Hebrews 11:6

> *In whom or what do you trust? Where do you place your faith?*

> *What personal pressures or disappointments affect your faith in God?*

> *Heavenly Father, help me recognize and resist distractions. You are trustworthy. May my faith in You no longer depend on the circumstances in the world or the personal struggles in my life.*

Make Your words sweet to my taste —
like honey. (Psalm 119:103)

December 4
21 Days til Christmas

No Chance

Luke 1:8-17

Zechariah: one priest in one division. Divisions so large the privilege to enter the temple might occur once in a lifetime. The casting of lots determined service — a lottery system — some never chosen. What we consider a game of chance, Scripture says "its every decision is from the Lord" (Proverbs 16:33). This day, God had a plan and purpose for Zechariah in the temple.

In the hushed temple, surrounded by prayer, Zechariah's work was interrupted by an angel of the Lord: *Your prayer for a son has been heard.* The angel revealed his son's name, his character, and his purpose. Nothing left to chance. Zechariah's son became known as John the Baptist who baptized with water, making way for the One who would baptize with the Holy Spirit and fire (Luke 3:15-18). Even before conception, God had a plan and purpose for the life of Zechariah's son.

Are the lives of Zechariah and his son a rare exception or is God intimately involved in every individual's life? The idea of a purposeful God involved in the everyday events of our lives seems unreasonable. Chance appears to be the fuel on which the world runs... a future spouse met because you stopped at Starbuck's on the way home... a wreck avoided because you couldn't find your keys... It's easier to believe in a universe whose origin is a random series of events rather than one created by the will of a purposeful and loving God. The idea of a God with so much power and purpose is too hard for us to wrap our finite minds around.

The thought of a God who has times, places, plans, and purposes for billions of people, over thousands of centuries, truly boggles my mind. *How can I relate to such a great God?* It's challenging for me to organize the timing of dinner so the baked potatoes are done before the chicken has turned to rubber and the peas require Botox. By faith Christians have to view the world from a different perspective. We cannot discount God's presence.

God has a plan and purpose for every individual.

> *"...From one man he made all the nations, that they should inhabit the whole earth; and he marked out their appointed times in history and the boundaries of their lands. God did this so that they would seek him and perhaps reach out for him and find him, though he is not far from any one of us. 'For in him we live and move and have our being.'..."*
> — Acts 17:26-28a

He had a plan and purpose for Zechariah... He had a plan and purpose for Zechariah's son... He has a plan and purpose for you... Whatever He allows is part of His plan for His purpose. There is no chance.

How does it make you feel to eliminate the idea of "chance" and replace it with the idea of God, who is in control of every event that ever happened or will happen?

Do you believe God has a plan and purpose for every happening in your life? Explain your answer.

Lord, help me to accept the reality of Your sovereign control, there is no "chance." Help me to see Your plan and purpose for my life.

God, help me to see Your Word as "eternal."
Show me how it fits into my world today and still
"stands firm in the heavens." (Psalm 119:89)

December 5
20 Days til Christmas

Seeing is Not Believing
Luke 1:18-20

Zechariah, in the middle of a supernatural event, could not see past his earthly circumstances. The angel of the Lord prophesied a son, the world revealed an old man with an old barren wife. Zechariah responded with unbelief.

Why did a man who lived faithfully in a chaotic culture struggle with unbelief? *What went wrong?* The world went wrong — it's broken. Zechariah was a product of his environment. The same one we inhabit. A world continually drawing our attention away from the supernatural unseen God of the universe, enticing us to believe only what we perceive with our senses and understand with our minds.

Zechariah underestimated the One he served. The radical message of life emerging from a dead womb was beyond belief. He couldn't hear the heavens declare the glory of God or the skies proclaim the work of His hands

(Psalm 19:1). He forgot the Lord he served was not bound by His own laws — nothing too hard for Him (Jeremiah 32:27). The heart of a faithful man became hardened to the most profound truth: God is God.

Believers are not immune to the lies of the world. They infect our souls and leave us with the consequences of unbelief. The angel gave Zechariah great news, but took the blessing of telling others. His voice silenced until everything came to pass...

The consequences of unbelief caught up with me in the form of anxiety, shortly after I began walking with Christ. I *thought* I believed, yet my response to anxiety and fear revealed something completely different. I didn't believe God was bigger than my worries or that He had my best interest at heart. I didn't believe in His sovereignty or His love for me. My doubt ran deep and my faith just skimmed the surface. Graciously, God slowly lifted me out of the pit as I repented, replacing lies with truth. I now recognize anxiety as the consequence of sinful unbelief and actively combat it with praise and repentance. I refuse to miss out on His blessing of peace anymore.

Every Believer is called to demonstrate truth to unbelievers through a life of faith. Before we try to convince others, we should take time to examine our own beliefs. Do your actions reflect a faithful life or one based on the ways of the world? The world encourages us to believe only what we see, while God defines faith as believing *without* seeing.

Now faith is confidence in what we hope for and assurance about what we do not see. — Hebrews 11:1

The depth of our faith directly affects our response to God and determines whether we live from a foundation of fear or hope, faith or doubt.

Do you have any beliefs that contradict God's Word? What are they?

How could your view of the world and your knowledge of God be limiting His work in your life?

Lord, please show me the areas of unbelief in my life and grow my faith so I may believe You without seeing. I do not want to miss Your blessing.

Father God, I want to feel Your face shine upon me as I read Your Word, but I confess: I do not have a servant's attitude. Bless me with a teachable heart. (Psalm 119:135)

December 6
19 Days til Christmas

Wonder Struck
Luke 1:21-25

God is God, He has no regard for the plans of mankind, He does whatever He pleases (Psalm 135:6). Likewise, most of us, Believers and unbelievers alike, fill our calendars and go about life without much regard for God's plan. Our days usually go as expected, but when the unexpected interferes we find ourselves in a state of wonder. Wondering what went wrong or wondering how such a blessing came to be. When you find yourself wondering, look for God.

God interrupted the worship service at the temple. The people's waiting turned to wondering. They expected Zechariah to emerge and give the traditional blessing, the one given since the time of Moses:

"The Lord bless you and keep you; the Lord make his face shine upon you and be gracious to

> *you; the Lord turn his face toward you and give you peace."* —Numbers 6:24-26

Instead, they received strange hand gestures. *What happened? Did the priest receive a vision? Was it good news or bad? Was he blessed or cursed?* God's plan took precedence and the worshipers wondered.

Elizabeth dealt with unmet expectations. Pregnant at her age... *unthinkable!* She couldn't share the news with her friends and neighbors. Who would believe? She spent the early months of her pregnancy wondering in amazement and sharing her joy with God. He poured out His favor on her and removed her disgrace. God interrupted Elizabeth's life and left her wondering.

In both instances, God's interruption turned the thoughts and minds of Believers to Himself. God upsets our plans to get our attention and teach us something we need to know about ourselves or Him. He disrupts our lives in order to include us in His plans. I'm familiar with God's interruptions...

Early in my walk with Christ, my marriage came to a difficult place. In my heart, I cried out to God: *Fix my husband!* In the middle of my heartfelt prayer, a Bible reference came to mind: book and chapter. My tears stopped. I grabbed my Bible... turning pages... wondering... *What will it say?* To loosely paraphrase, it read: *Change yourself and the change in you will affect your husband* (1Peter 3). Immediately, my wonder turned from awe to frustration. *What? You want me to change?* God interrupted with specific instructions, turning my attention toward Him in more ways than one.

God disrupts the plans of Believers and unbelievers alike. From daily challenges to unimaginable blessings, any interruption in our lives leaves us wondering. The next time you find yourself in a state of wonder, look for signs of God's plan. Good or bad — God works His plans into our lives for His purpose and our good.

Recall the last time you were left wondering and consider that God interrupted your life. What was He trying to teach you?

_____

Heavenly Father, You are a God of wonder. Please turn my thoughts to you the next time I find myself wondering.

_____

*Heavenly Father, You feel so far away, show
me You are near. Your ways are so different
than the world's ways, show me they are true.
Open my heart to You.* (Psalm 119:151)

December 7
18 Days til Christmas

Known

Luke 1:26-38

God knew Mary, where she lived, her family and her fiancé, but most importantly, He knew her heart.

> *But if anyone loves God, he is known by God.*
> —1Corinthians 8:3 (ESV)

God knows those who love Him, and those who love Him obey Him (1John 5:3). God knew Mary to be a faithful, obedient young woman — one He could trust with a difficult call.

Mary's encounter with the angel Gabriel filled her with fear. Not an uncommon emotion when one of God's angels shows up. Yet, I doubt Gabriel's words of comfort calmed her for long. Mary received a calling that gave her fear a legitimate basis.

Gabriel told Mary — a virgin pledged to be married — she would become an unwed mother. If Mary said Yes to God, her world would be turned upside down. The culture she lived in would assume she had been involved in an adulterous affair, which meant public humiliation, certain rejection from her fiancé, and disgrace for her family. Submission to God's call put her entire future at stake. It was a *fear-full* risk.

In the face of fear, Mary simply responded: "I am the Lord's servant... May your word to me be fulfilled." Mary loved God more than she loved herself or her world. She chose to obey, despite fear and the potential for great personal loss.

Fear's powerful grip can become an obstacle that keeps Believers from doing what they know is right. God doesn't often call us to risk our entire future for Him. We live in a society where the faith of a Believer can be practiced with relative safety. The biggest risks God calls me to take involve putting my ego on the line. Facing head on the fear of dying from embarrassment, rejection, or humiliation. Perhaps God doesn't call me to anything greater because He knows I'm not ready — He knows the limits of my love for Him...

Jesus revealed the most important commandment: "Love the Lord your God with all your heart and with all your soul and with all your mind and with all your strength" (Mark 12:30). Just maybe, God's desire for us to know Him and glorify Him with our lives caused Him to place this command in its preeminent position. He wants to be able to call on us to work with Him, but if our hearts, minds, and souls are more concerned about personal safety than loving God we won't be given an opportunity to be the Lord's servant.

God calls those He knows. Mary's response did not surprise Him. He also knows exactly how you and I might respond to His call. Don't miss the incredible opportunity and privilege of serving the Lord. Choose to love Him. Be known.

And this is love: that we walk in obedience to his commands. — 2John 6

When was the last time God called you to demonstrate your love for Him?

What would it take for you to be able to answer like Mary: "May your word to me be fulfilled…"?

_____

Lord, grow me to love You with all my heart, soul, mind, and strength — I want You to know me.

_____

Almighty God, teach me to "eat" Your words. Make them my joy and my heart's delight. (Jeremiah 15:16)

December 8
17 Days til Christmas

The Un-Common Tie that Binds

Luke 1:39-45

Mary found herself alone, filled with fear and excitement. *Who could she share this experience with? Who would understand?* The people closest to her (parents, fiancé, neighbors) would not be thrilled with the news of her pregnancy. From a worldly perspective, virgins are *never* pregnant. She needed a friend, someone who had personal experience with the miraculous ways of God, someone who would believe her.

The angel's message to Mary included the news of her cousin Elizabeth's pregnancy (Luke 1:36). God prepared the way for Mary to be blessed with support during this time of waiting — Elizabeth would understand. Mary wasted no time in getting to her cousin's house.

The reunion of these two women bore the mark of a supernatural bond. An unlikely connection given their age difference: Elizabeth, married for decades, years of joy and heartache; Mary, a young bride-to-be, waiting for her wedding day. They could have been from different generations. Yet, by the power of the Holy Spirit, Mary's simple greeting conveyed to Elizabeth all that had transpired. Together they celebrated, encouraged in each other's presence. No generation gap, just a bond of love and understanding.

I'm privileged to have lots of cousins in a wide range of ages. Outside of aunts and uncles, we haven't always had common ground on which to connect. As a teen, I had more fun interacting with their children. Now that I'm a mother of teens, they are grandmothers. Over the years, God has created opportunities for me to come to know some of these wonderful women as sisters in Christ, adding depth and intimacy to our relationships. If your family tree is short on branches, don't feel left out, God provides all Believers with a large family. It's called the Church.

Sometimes, I marvel at the people God has placed in my life through the Church. I've seen the power of the Holy Spirit build bridges across the generation gap, the socioeconomic gap, the race gap, the political gap, and the personality gap. Rich relationships seemingly built on nothing. The Holy Spirit connects Believers in a unique way, something unbelievers cannot experience. As we witnessed between Elizabeth and Mary, the bond of Christian fellowship goes beyond social interaction. Fellowship shares and celebrates God's work in our lives, a relationship enhanced by the presence of the Spirit. In fellowship we receive encouragement, affirmation, and insight regarding our faith journey.

Mary, carrying the Son of God, overflowed with the Holy Spirit; her presence had a profound effect on Elizabeth. Every Christian has the supernatural activity of the Spirit at work in their life. As we share our God-experiences and insights with others, true fellowship prepares the way for spiritual growth. *Are you in a spiritual rut?* Ask God to provide someone to come alongside you in fellowship. Keep your eyes and heart open. It will probably be someone unexpected.

Do you have a Christian friend, or a group of Believers you can fellowship with? If not, consider the people in your life. Ask God to guide you to the one who also desires a Christ-centered relationship.

Holy Spirit, help me to recognize opportunities for fellowship.

December 9
16 Days til Christmas

A Proper Perspective

Luke 1:46-56

Uncertainty… it brings most of us to our knees in doubt and despair. Yet Mary cried out:

My soul glorifies the Lord and my spirit rejoices in God my Savior…

Looking into an uncertain future, Mary praised God with joy! Her unique response flowed from a God-centered heart. She saw through the eyes of a humble servant wholly dependent on her Master whose love never fails, whose thoughts and judgment descend from an eternal perspective of righteousness and perfection.

The Greek translated as *glorifies* literally means "to make great, magnify" (Enhanced Strong's Lexicon). A life that glorifies God, magnifies GOD. Mary exalted Him above herself and joyfully placed her future in His hands. Her song of praise revealed a rich knowledge of

God's faithful history with His people. Truths she learned from His Word.

God meets us in the pages of Scripture when we approach it with a prayerful and expectant heart. Studying, meditating on, and memorizing God's Word builds the framework for a deep relationship with Him and leads to first-hand experiential knowledge of our heavenly Father. Humbled in His presence, we gain a proper perspective — looking up from bended knee. His Word helps us understand and accept the reality of who He is and, in the process, highlights the sin of pride in our lives.

Webster's defines *pride* as "having or displaying excessive self-esteem." Pride focuses on *self-magnification*, leaving little room for God in the view-finder. We no longer see God or glorify Him, it's all about SELF. God loves us too much to leave us blind to the truth, especially when it saves us from destruction. He works in the lives of the proud to correct their vision: *God opposes the proud but gives grace to the humble* (James 4:6).

God's cure for pride: affliction (Isaiah 48:10, 11). Affliction comes in as many different forms and degrees as the varying personalities whose lives they enter, each with the power to reveal inadequacies and frailties. God lovingly brings us to the point where we cry to Him for help, but it is not God's heart to hurt us (Lamentations 3:33). Physical diseases often require painful treatment; the same is true for spiritual ailments.

One of my most painful afflictions came through the illness and death of my mom. During this difficult time, God became very LARGE. Through the pain, I began to understand my dependence on Him. My perspective changed regarding God's place in my life. This experience became a life-defining moment — singular in its importance.

God is the *only* One to be glorified. Without Him we are nothing. Everything we have comes from Him: possessions... talents... the next beat of our heart... The more we comprehend our true dependence on God, the more contentment we experience. Develop a servant's heart and discover a joyful spirit. Mary's song of praise should be ours as well. After all, we have *nothing* to offer God except what He has provided. *Who are we that He should be mindful of us?*

Humble yourselves before the Lord, and he will lift you up. — James 4:10

Do you see yourself as self-reliant or humbly dependent?

Do you know the joy of being a humble servant of the Lord? Explain.

Lord, help me to gain a proper perspective of who You truly are.

God, You say Your Word is flawless, help me to see the truth. As I test Your Word in my life, be my Shield. (Proverbs 30:5)

December 10
15 Days til Christmas

Alone

Luke 1:57-61

The angel's words came true — Elizabeth and Zechariah became the parents of a baby boy. Neighbors and family shared in their joy. At the proper time, they gathered to celebrate the new addition to their faith community. Jewish law required all baby boys to be ceremonially circumcised on the eighth day of their birth.

Circumcision represents faith in God's promises. God established the practice through a covenant with Abraham, the father of our faith (Romans 4:9-12). The promise included God's blessing on Abraham and his descendants, along with the commitment to grow them into many nations (Genesis 17). The act of circumcision confirms the Jews' trust in the covenant promise and reminds them they are to live for God and not the world.

Zechariah remained tongue-tied on the occasion of his son's circumcision. Those conducting the service prepared to name the baby after his father. Elizabeth boldly objected. Clearly, she had not been consulted beforehand about the baby's name, after all that responsibility belonged to the father and he was mute. She surprised everyone present by speaking up, challenging their authority, and choosing a seemingly random name. Elizabeth defied tradition, culture, and peer pressure to do what she knew to be right. She stood alone against the toughest audience of all: family, friends, and religious leaders. Elizabeth demonstrated her faithfulness to God beautifully.

As followers of Christ, we are to disregard the influence of family, friends, and society when their counsel contradicts God's. We have to be willing to stand firm and resist peer pressure — a forceful influence, no matter our age. Adults face the same challenges as children and teens. Consider:

How did you respond the last time a conversation turned to gossip? Did you join in? Did you listen? Did you walk away?

What about the last crude joke you heard? Did you wait for the punch-line? Did you tell it to a friend?

Last time you ate out with friends or co-workers, were you embarrassed to offer a prayer of thanks before eating?

These examples may seem trivial, but they are not trivial to God. Gossip is sin (Romans 1:29). Dirty jokes, sin (Ephesians 5:3-4). Being ashamed of God, also sin (Luke

9:26). God does not take sin lightly — He died for our sins.

Believers are called to be holy. Set apart for God — choosing God's way, not the socially acceptable way. Like Elizabeth, sometimes we have to stand alone... By the way, one day, you alone will answer to God for the choices you make.

For we must all appear before the judgment seat of Christ, so that each of us may receive what is due us for the things done while in the body, whether good or bad. —2Corinthians 5:10

Are you willing to stand alone for Christ?

What was the last opportunity you had to be faithful to God? How did you respond?

_____

Father, forgive me for every time I have given in to peer pressure. Only in Your strength can I choose to stand firm for Your way.

_____

Your words, O Lord, are flawless. Reveal the flaws in my thinking that hinder belief and obstruct understanding. (Psalm 12:6)

December 11
14 Days til Christmas

Praise the Lord!
Luke 1:62-66

Make-shift sign language... a writing tablet... *His name is John...* a loosed tongue of praise... a sense of awe... An ordinary celebration for an unexpected blessing transformed into a wondrous revelation. Praise flipped the switch, bringing the truth to light.

All around us the ordinary longs to be recognized for what it truly is — extraordinary — a planet teeming with awesome events, *every* birth a miracle. Any effort spent contemplating our world — its complexity, magnitude, and sheer genius — exposes the hand of the Creator: *His invisible qualities clearly seen from what has been made* (Romans 1:20). Yet, we walk around preoccupied and desensitized to the evidence of the divine wonder surrounding us. Living, growing, thriving in an environment we could never have created for ourselves.

The Israelites entered a promised land they had no hand in establishing. Moses told them: "When you have eaten and are satisfied, praise the Lord your God for the good land he has given you" (Deuteronomy 8:10). Surrounded by abundance, protected by God's blessing, the Israelites would become proud if they neglected to honor God with praise. Pride would lead to destruction, just as it did the nations whose land they now inhabited. Praise opens our eyes to the truth.

Believers most often associate praise with Sunday worship, only praise is for every day — *as often as we eat and are satisfied*. The prayer ministry of Moms In Prayer International[3] taught me the practice of praise. It has become my favorite part of prayer. As I praise God, He seems to reflect the truth of who He is back into my spirit, building confidence in His character and strengthening faith.

During a particular season, I became captivated by the notion of God as Creator. Praise caused the world to become a marvel to me. One day driving home, I began to see things in a new light. Everything shimmered with His glory... trees... houses... streets... cars... *everything...* Colossians 1:17 became visible: "He is before all things, and in Him all things hold together."

Zechariah's praise revealed God's work in the odd, but ordinary, circumstances surrounding his family. Awe and wonder spread throughout the countryside. Praise

---

3 Moms In Prayer International is an inter-denominational ministry that encourages moms to gather one hour a week to pray for their children, their schools, their teachers and administrators. For more information go to www.momsinprayer.org.

can do the same for you. Practice a life of praise and see the One holding it all together. Turn your life into an awesome event. Praise the Lord!

Have you practiced praising God in your daily life?

Do you recognize God's work in your world — do you even think to look for it?

Lord, open the eyes of my heart so I may see Your awesome work in the world around me. Teach me to praise Your name.

Heavenly Father, I confess, I don't understand
Your ways. Open my eyes, enable me to see
wonderful things in Your law. (Psalm 119:18)

December 12
13 Days til Christmas

Spiritually Speaking
Luke 1:67-75

Zechariah, filled with the Holy Spirit, began to prophesy — *declaring that which can only be known by divine revelation* (Enhanced Strong's Lexicon). Divine revelation comes from God alone. He imparts knowledge and understanding, words and wisdom, unattainable any other way.

The perspective unique.

Praise be to the Lord... he has come and has redeemed his people.

The Lord has **redeemed** his people — the Greek is translated as *past tense.* A prophetic perspective, for at this moment our Redeemer still dwelt in His mother's womb. Zechariah declared a truth invisible to everyone but God who sees from His eternal perspective. *This is divine knowledge.*

The purpose proclaimed.

> *He has raised up a horn of salvation for us in the house of his servant David... to show mercy to our fathers and to remember his holy covenant, the oath he swore to our father Abraham...*

A horn of salvation, the symbol of the powerful savior God promised would come from the line of King David (Psalm 89:19-29). The oath He swore to Abraham, spiritual father of the faithful, promised a blessing for all people through his offspring (Genesis 22:17-18). Zechariah's prophetic message proclaimed fulfillment of these promises: Jesus. *This is divine understanding.*

Prior to Christ's resurrection, few people had the privilege of experiencing the power of the Holy Spirit to proclaim a prophetic message. At this extraordinary time in history, God gave Zechariah the perfect words to share with family and friends for His purpose, yet I doubt anyone understood what they heard. Apart from the Spirit, our understanding is limited.

Believers, each indwelt by the Holy Spirit, possess the potential to speak and understand divine revelation. Only by the power of the Spirit can we share godly words of wisdom with others and interpret God's Word in a way that enriches our lives and guides our steps. I know there have been times in my life when the Spirit provided the right words for the occasion.

My mother-in-law's graveside service was coming to an end when my sister-in-law asked me to pray. Ordinarily, such a spontaneous request would have triggered a wave of anxiety, but my spirit was calm and I accepted the offer to pray. We gathered in a circle holding hands, many unbelievers present to memorialize the life of a Believer. I remember few occasions when a prayer flowed so freely and easily, laced with God's Word and the truth of salvation through His Son. I trust the Spirit provided the exact words for His purpose and for the moment — I know they weren't mine.

The Holy Spirit speaks through and to Believers, provides understanding of God's Word, and reveals truth to our hearts. If you are willing and open to Him, He will give you the right words at the proper time, making you a conduit for *divine knowledge and understanding.*

We have been rescued… so we can serve God without fear, in holiness and righteousness for as long as we live. – Luke 1:74-75 (NLT)

What does it mean to you to have access to the Holy Spirit "24/7"?

Do you believe He might want to speak to others through you? Why or why not?

Bless me with the boldness and faith to allow the Holy Spirit to speak through me to others.

Lord, teach me to meditate and consider
Your ways. May I find joy in Your Word, so
I won't neglect it. (Psalm 119:15-16)

December 13
12 Days til Christmas

The Path to Peace

Luke 1:76-80

Zechariah's prophetic song continues. The focus switched to his newborn son, John.

> *And you, my child, will be called a prophet of*
> *the Most High; for you will go on before the Lord to*
> *prepare the way for him...*

John became known as John the Baptist, the one voice calling in the desert: *Repent!* (Matthew 3). Repentance prepares the way for a hard-heart to receive Jesus — the Prince of Peace — as Lord.

Repenting involves a painful process: recognition of sin, turning from it, and realizing the need for forgiveness. Admitting sin requires a setting aside of pride when we would much rather make excuses, justify actions, and/or assign blame than confess wrong-doing. Then once we have lowered ourselves to recognize sin, we must turn from it. Turning from sin may be more difficult than confession; after all, sin is tempting. The final step involves asking for forgiveness, an extremely humbling experience. The arduous work of repentance softens hardened-hearts and prepares the way for peace.

God, in His tender mercy, continues to send the message of repentance into the world through His Spirit — the Counselor (John 16:7-8). Separated from Him by sin, He knows we live in darkness and walk in the shadow of death. Until we recognize our need for a Savior, we will reject salvation. Without salvation, we have no peace.

It seems odd to consider something as painful as repentance leading to peace. Confession, submission, and humbly asking for forgiveness sound like ways to increase pain in your life. However, after accepting Christ's gift of salvation, the power and grace of the Holy Spirit guide us onto the path of peace. Reconciliation with God through repentance secures the inner tranquility and joy we all seek.

The conversion experience is not a one-time event — a box to be checked — pouring out sins and receiving forgiveness. Our initial conversion marks a new life and a new journey. The way God has planned for us generates a changed heart, not just forgiveness. He patiently works in our lives exposing sinful habits and thought patterns previously unrecognized. Strongholds embedded so deeply we don't see them.

In my own life, God has revealed new facets of being judgmental, arrogant, and deceitful. I had no idea! Each new realization requires the painful process of repentance: confession, submission, and forgiveness. Yet, as I obediently submit to God in dealing with sin, I experience new levels of deliverance and peace.

God's call is still the same: *Repent!* The Hebrew literally means *return, turn around* (Dictionary of Biblical Languages). Our Creator paid a high price to make the way for people to return to Him through Jesus. He desires everyone to come to repentance (2Peter 3:9) and receive His peace. You may be missing out on day to day peace because you are an unrepentant sinner. Invite God to examine your life, come into agreement with Him, and allow Him to guide your feet onto the path of peace.

Search me, O God, and know my heart; test me and know my anxious thoughts. Point out anything in me that offends you, and lead me in the path of everlasting life. — Psalm 139:23-24 NLT

Are you at peace: with God? ...with others? ...with yourself?

Dear Lord, help me to examine my heart for unrepentant sin, prepare my heart for confession and obedience. I want to know Your peace.

Heavenly Father, teach me to "eat" Your Word
so I might truly live. (Matthew 4:4)

December 14
11 Days til Christmas

Righteous Dilemmas

Matthew 1:18-21

Joseph faced a heart-rending discovery requiring a difficult decision. He carefully weighed his options, wrestled his emotions, and resolved to quietly divorce Mary.

In Jewish culture, the pledge of marriage was a legally binding agreement requiring a divorce decree to be broken. Joseph did not want to disgrace Mary. He wanted to keep the whole distressing affair quiet. She and her family would face enough trouble with a baby on the way. His combination of righteousness and compassion should not surprise us — God chose Joseph as carefully as He chose Mary.

A righteous man, Joseph considered divorce the only option. However, God intervened with an alternative plan:

... take Mary home as your wife...

God asked Joseph to set aside *his* righteousness — a strict keeping of the law — and take a pregnant woman as his wife. Joseph knew the child was not his. He knew this option God proposed would expose both him and Mary to gossip, judgment, and public disgrace. Joseph had a new decision to make: trust God or succumb to social pressure and save his own reputation.

God challenged Joseph's definition of righteousness, in the same way Jesus challenged the righteousness of the teachers of the law and the Pharisees. Righteousness depends on trusting the Law-maker not our own understanding of the law. Abraham was credited with righteousness because he believed God (Romans 4:3). Jesus exposed the hearts of the Pharisees as empty and dead — compassionless — focused on self-righteousness rather than the heart of the law (Matthew 23:27, 28).

Self-righteousness blinds us to true righteousness. We become judgmental and more concerned with others' opinions of us than caring for others. We no longer embrace our sinful past (or present) and forget that God does His best work with the broken. We forget Jesus came "not to call the righteous, but sinners..." (Luke 5:31-32). Only God knows what goes on in a person's heart — He alone knows the truly righteous.

Two books have challenged me with accounts of godly men who did not fit the stereotype of Christian culture. *Same Kind of Different as Me* tells the story of an uneducated homeless man, a modern-day prophet, whom God uses to bring about significant social change in the city where he lives. The other book, *Dirty Word,* includes the story of a tattoo artist, heavily tattooed and pierced, who "hosts a 24/7 prayer chapel in the basement of his home." Both radical disciples of Christ, both with messy looking lives. Could you accept these men if they crossed your path? Could I?

Sometimes God asks us to get involved with people whose lives look messy. Like Joseph, we have a decision to make: Do we obey God, risking our reputations? Or do we protect our image? Maybe we should make the *righteous* decision and trust God, His perspective, and His work. Things aren't always what they appear to be.

What is your definition of "righteousness": a strict keeping of the law OR faith in God?

Do you trust God enough to lay down your life, your reputation, and your pride for Him? Explain.

*Heavenly Father help me to be willing to put aside **my** reputation and **my** righteousness and trust You to guide me when I am faced with the "messy" lives of others.*

Your Word, Lord, is like the rain, when it comes down it does not return to heaven without "watering" the earth and causing growth. May Your Word fulfill Your purpose in my life. (Isaiah 44:10-11)

December 15
10 Days til Christmas

Grounded in the Word

Matthew 1:22-25

At Joseph's critical turning point, Matthew interrupts the story with commentary:

> *All this took place to fulfill what the Lord had said through the prophet...*

Matthew's Jewish audience referred to their Bible — the Old Testament — as *the Law and the Prophets*[4]. They immediately understood the importance of this interjection: *Here's evidence of God's plan and promise being fulfilled.* Joseph, as a righteous man, grounded his life in God's Word.

---

4 New International Version Study Bible 1984, note on Matthew 5:17.

The angel's message (Matthew 1:20-21) provided Joseph with the information needed to understand he was being called to be the earthly father of the Messiah — the promised Savior:

Joseph son of David... The Savior would be from the family line of King David.

...what is conceived in her is from the Holy Spirit... A virgin will give birth to the Messiah.

...give him the name Jesus... A name that means "the Lord saves."

The very verse Matthew referenced may have echoed in Joseph's heart as he awoke...

The virgin will conceive and will give birth to a son, and will call him Immanuel. —Isaiah 7:14

Joseph's knowledge of God's Word combined with the divine message helped him know what to do... *When Joseph woke up, he took Mary home as his wife.*

Jesus told His disciples the Holy Spirit would come and remind them of everything He had said (John 14:26). Jesus — the Word made flesh (John 1:14) — is God. Therefore, the sum of "the Law and the Prophets" plus the New Testament are *His* words. Knowing the Bible in its entirety gives the Holy Spirit tools to work with when providing guidance to a Believer. Of course, the opposite is true too, He can't remind us of what we have never heard (or read).

Scripture is essential to our relationship with God. By the power of the Holy Spirit, He speaks to us through His Word, providing direction, discipline, and encouragement. Make time to meet with God in the pages of the Bible every day. Open your Bible with a prayer asking the Spirit to show you what you need to know. Be expectant and patient as you begin. It takes time to learn His voice. Walking with God daily in His Word prepares you for whatever the future holds, and builds your faith and trust in Him.

"In this world you will have trouble" (John 16:33), only time separates us from the next emotionally draining and difficult trial. Decisions often need to be made quickly. Get ready now. Joseph's knowledge of Scripture and his willingness to let it guide him helped him make the right choice.

I have hidden your word in my heart that I might not sin against you. — Psalm 119:11

Ground yourself in God's Word. The Holy Spirit will remind you when you need it most.

Are you acquiring tools the Holy Spirit can use to help you make the right decision in confusing times? Why or why not?

Lord, fill me with a desire for Your Word and teach me to hide it in my heart. Enable me to make the right decision with the guidance of the Holy Spirit.

*Heavenly Father, when I read Your Word turn
my questions and confusion into a prayer. Bless
me with understanding.* (Psalm 119:169)

December 16
9 Days til Christmas

Divine Orchestration

Luke 2:1-7

Caesar Augustus, the greatest of the Roman emperors,
led this Empire to its peak influence in the world. His
rule marked the beginning of a 200 year period of peace
— the *Pax Romana* — which gave the world time to
create advances in travel, communication, philosophy,
and artistic pursuits.[5] Advancements which prepared the
world for Jesus.

The emperor's census required every citizen to register
in the town of their ancestral origin.[6] Joseph and Mary
belonged to the lineage of King David whose birthplace
was Bethlehem. The call to travel and the timing of
the census resulted in the fulfillment of a 700 year old

---

5 Lagass, Paul and Columbia University. *The Columbia Encyclopedia.*
      6th ed. New York; Detroit: Columbia University Press; Sold
      and distributed by Gale Group, 2000.
6 New International Version Study Bible 1984 note, Luke 2:3

prophecy (Micah 5:2) — the Messiah's birth in Bethlehem. Fulfilled prophecy, a hallmark of God, testifies to the authenticity of Jesus as the Messiah. Through a Roman emperor and an Old Testament prophet, God provided a way for the world to identify His Son.

The *Pax Romana* continued well after Caesar Augustus' death, preparing avenues for the Gospel to spread. Most of the world spoke a common language under Roman rule giving news an opportunity to circulate rapidly. A nation at peace gave people time to turn their hearts and minds toward the arts and philosophy, rather than war and survival. An extensive system of roads was developed during this period making way for a postal service to be established, helping evangelists like Paul travel and Christian leaders communicate with fledgling churches. The world was accessible to those who had the Good News, both mentally and physically.

God prepared the world on a large scale to receive His Son, but He works on a smaller scale too, in individual lives like mine. God encourages me through books by authors living and dead. At just the right time and place, the needed insight comes to me through their words. Once, it was a book I had put down for several months, one I felt guilty about not finishing. Yet the next time I opened it, waiting for news of my father in an ICU waiting room, there were the perfect words for my situation. It was as if God spoke directly to me. *Did He inspire an author years earlier just for me? How did He get the book into my hand on that day, on that page?* It could only be God.

God in His Sovereignty works out events without regard to time and space, engineering His purpose over the ages. It boggles the mind to think of the orchestration required to prepare the way for Jews and Gentiles to pay attention to the Good News (or for me to get those books)... With God all things are possible — both large and small.

Do you believe that it was just good timing that Jesus was born during this period of history?

OR

Do you believe God is constantly orchestrating all the world's events in order to fulfill His purpose? Explain.

_____

God, fill me with the wonder and truth of Your power to work all things for Your purpose through Believers and unbelievers alike.

_____

God, Your every word is flawless. Instill this truth in my heart and teach me to take refuge in You. (Proverbs 30:5)

December 17
8 Days til Christmas

Conditional Peace

Luke 2:8-14

The shepherds living out in the fields had little to no influence in the world around them. Only sheep listened to them — not the most likely candidates to receive the angelic message of great joy for all people. Priests, rabbis, or kings maybe, but not shepherds. *Why would God choose lowly herdsmen to be the first to hear of His Son's birth?* Because God doesn't see people the way we do — He sees their hearts.

> *People look at the outward appearance, but the Lord looks at the heart.* — 1Samuel 16:7

God knew the hearts of the shepherds. Watching over their flocks at great personal risk, He saw men focused on others more than themselves. They were vulnerable to the elements, predators, and thieves. No city wall for protection, no guards watching over them. Being Jewish shepherds, they trusted God for protection. Maybe they sang Psalm 23 as they worked: "The Lord is my Shepherd, I shall not want..." What God saw pleased Him and He blessed them with the privilege of receiving the heavenly birth announcement.

God blesses everyone who pleases Him. The angels sang:

> *Glory to God in the highest heaven, and on earth* **peace to those on whom his favor rests.** (Emphasis added.)

The blessing of God's favor is peace, only it's not a peace dependent on a life free from difficulties. God offers a deep peace of the soul and spirit, present even when your world falls apart. A heart trusting in Jesus Christ as Lord receives the blessing of God's peace.

Trusting Jesus — day by day, moment by moment — requires a series of decisions to choose Him as the focus of your life. Some days, I look at all I have to do and become overwhelmed with anxiety. There isn't enough time in the day. All I see is me. But choosing to refocus on Who I belong to, His presence, and the truth that apart from Him I can do nothing (John 5:15), peace fills my heart. Now don't get me wrong, this is *not* easy. I have to choose to see with eyes of faith and surrender my day and all I have to do to Jesus, my Lord.

> *"I am the Lord your God, who teaches you what is best for you, who directs you in the way you should go. If only you had paid attention to my commands, your peace would be like a river..."*
> —Isaiah 48:17-18

My days flow peacefully when I submit to God and His way, anxiety subsides and time seems to multiply.

God favors those who receive His Son as Lord and blesses them with peace, no matter their social standing — shepherd or king. God doesn't look at accomplishments or status. He looks at who you are and what is important to you... God sees your heart.

What does God see when He looks in your heart: trust or anxiety?

Would you consider trusting Jesus as the Lord of your day, moment by moment? Why or why not?

Jesus, teach me to fully surrender to You as Lord. Remind me to choose to trust You when I am overwhelmed by anxiety. I want to know Your peace.

Lord, Your Word says You are gracious and righteous, full of compassion. Reveal this truth to me, sometimes it's hard for me to see. (Psalm 116:5)

December 18
7 Days til Christmas

Participation Required

Luke 2:15-20

A single moment in time... a message from heaven... a revelation from God... The shepherds stood in the same dark field but nothing was the same. Their response: *Let's go and see...* These men of the field chose to experience the message they received.

Experiencing the truth of revelation — hearing *and* seeing — increased the shepherds' faith, it was all true. They could not contain their newfound knowledge and shared it with everyone they met. *Participation in the revelation of God's Word increases faith and encourages us to witness to others.*

Everyone who heard the story was amazed. Mary treasured the shepherds' visit and their words — she stored the memory in her heart. The realities of pregnancy surely dampened the thrill of giving birth to the Messiah. The night-time visitors and their story of angels reminded

Mary of God's faithfulness. *Participation in the revelation of God's Word encourages His people.*

The shepherds' bold response to the revelation brought about an additional blessing: experiential knowledge of God and His character. They experienced His command of supernatural beings, His work through the lives of the humble, and His faithfulness. Their new knowledge burst forth in praise! *Participating in the revelation of God's Word leads to a deeper understanding of God's character and produces a heart of worship.*

Angels are not God's only messengers of revelation — He uses Scripture, His Spirit, and people. The most significant revelation I've received came through my mom via my brother. Her death seemed imminent when he brought her words out of ICU: *I trust, I trust.* Words revealing a God trustworthy in the face of death, a source of comfort and peace. A compassionate God who loved and cared for my mom — a life-changing revelation. In response, I began to live for God, seeking His way and following to the best of my understanding.

After seventeen years of participation, I have seen and experienced the truths exemplified by the shepherds. My faith has increased. To my amazement, God has used my witness to encourage others. I continue to grow a deeper understanding of God's character, which fills my heart with praise. What we see in the shepherds is still true today: *Participation in revelation impacts God's kingdom.*

When God reveals His Word in a new way, choose to participate. The shepherds could have stayed in the dark field, they did not have to *go and see...* Follow the shepherds to Bethlehem, participate in the revelation.

How do you respond to God's revelation?

Are you in the dark when it comes to God's Word? Explain.

OR

Have you participated in the revelation of God's Word? How?

Heavenly Father, reveal Your Word to me in a new way. I want to participate in Your kingdom.

*Heavenly Father, I deceive myself when I listen
to Your Word but do not do what it says — show
me how to live Your Word.* (James 1:22)

December 19
6 Days til Christmas

A Matter of the Heart

Luke 2:21-24

Mary and Joseph revealed their heart for God by obeying
a difficult call despite personal sacrifice. For this young
couple, following the Law was a simple act of love.

*I delight to do your will, O my God; Your law
is within my heart.* — Psalm 40:8 (ESV)

The Law invaded their hearts.

The ritual circumcision of their son became an
intimate occasion far beyond a reminder of God's covenant
with the Jewish patriarch Abraham — *God named this
baby.* The birds sacrificed revealed the humble position
of the family, they could not afford a lamb — *God's grace
magnified as He entrusted them with His Son.* Mary and
Joseph's obedience to God's call transformed their list of
religious obligations into a gift from the heart.

God could have entrusted the Messiah to any number of wealthy rabbis or Pharisees, but their hearts were not open to Him. During His ministry, Jesus exposed their character: *...they do not practice what they preach... Everything they do is done for men to see... hypocrites... whitewashed tombs...* (Matthew 23). Like so many, they used religion for personal gain and would not have sacrificed their reputations or their lives for God. In contrast, Mary and Joseph had hearts prepared to receive and obey a divine calling.

I confess, I grew up un-churched and began attending church primarily out of parental obligation — it was all about my children and the responsibility I felt to make sure they experienced church. I certainly didn't have a heart prepared to hear God or sacrifice my personal comfort for anything He might ask of me. However, a moment came when God captured my heart, from that point on nothing was the same.

Externally my life looked the same, only on the inside everything was different. I went to church for God, not my children. He was not forgotten Monday through Saturday — every day I talked to Him in prayer and looked for Him in the pages of my Bible. It became personal. My relationship with God grew. I began to hear His call, offering opportunities to prove my love with obedience.

God's intervention in my life was timed perfectly, my children were all under the age of five. By His grace, they have been raised in a home where religion is based on love, not obligation. The blessing of a real relationship with God far outweighs anything the world has to offer.

God didn't choose a wealthy family who could give Jesus prestige and everything money could buy. The family He chose provided what really mattered: a model of love for God. As Jesus grew, He watched His parents fulfill their personal call from God by lovingly and obediently raising Him according to the Law of the Lord. These are the qualities God looks for in the families of all His children. Evaluate your religion: *Is it a set of rules or a growing relationship?* Make way for the Law of the Lord to invade your heart.

Do you practice religion out of love? Explain.

Have you ever experienced a personal call from God? How did you respond?

Lord, I confess I don't love You as I should. Help me to remember, obedience to Your Word is an expression of love.

Lord, Your Word says You are good and all You do is good,
but in this world it's hard to believe. Help me to know
You as Good — teach me Your way. (Psalm 119:68)

December 20
5 Days til Christmas

Looking Forward
Luke 2:25-38

God brought two to the temple who recognized Jesus as the Messiah. Two who looked forward: Simeon saw *the consolation of Israel*, Anna saw *the redemption of Jerusalem*, all in the eyes of the Babe. An unanticipated encouragement for these young parents — affirmation of God's word — their unexpected child seen as the expected Savior who would bring comfort, redemption, and relief from sin for God's people. Except not everyone would see and be comforted. Simeon warned Mary...

> *"This child is destined to cause the falling and rising of many in Israel, and to be a sign that will be spoken against... hearts will be revealed. And a sword will pierce your own soul too."*

...Jesus's future included suffering, and so did hers.

The Redeemer entered a world at war — a battle waging for the hearts of individuals, since the beginning (Genesis 2-3). Satan's successful deception of the ones God created for His glory turned hearts from good to evil, light to dark, freedom to slavery. The ongoing deceit prevents most from seeing the war or even knowing they have taken sides. Jesus came to open the eyes of the blind, reveal truth, and set captives free (Luke 4:18-21).

Unfortunately, those blinded to the truth see no need for a Savior. They do not consider themselves captives and take offense at such a notion (John 8:31-33). Reactions vary from mild indignation or irritation to cruel condescension or rage. The battle's point of greatest intensity culminates in the church, exactly where Jesus entered. Powerful Jewish religious leaders — deceived, legalistic and self-righteous — unwittingly fell in line with Satan (John 8:42-47). Jesus's message filled them with fear and anger, not comfort. They fought against Him. The battle ended at a cross... Jesus crucified... dead... buried... and Mary's heart... pierced by the suffering of her son.

Motivated by love, Jesus came to die for our sins. Rather than letting us suffer the righteous consequences of our own rebellion, He became our righteousness (1Corinthians 1:30). He freely offers the gift of salvation to anyone who believes. Believers trust Him enough to follow, and those who follow Him suffer (John 15:20). There was a time when I willfully chose not to follow, seeing clearly where His painful path led. I looked forward, but not far enough. Once I got a glimpse of the glory beyond the cross — the resurrection and eternal life — my perspective lengthened. I saw farther down the road and began to understand how He uses suffering for good and the salvation of others. Yes, following Christ comes with a cost, only that's not the whole story: *On the third day He was raised to life!*

Looking forward we see the potential for suffering as we follow Jesus, and yes, He actually calls to us: *Take up your cross.* However, there is an awaited glory! Simeon and Anna both possessed the gift of faith enabling them to look beyond what the world revealed. They saw the Messiah in a baby — the coming consolation and redemption of God's people. Look forward…

> *For just as we share abundantly in the sufferings of Christ, so also our comfort abounds through Christ.* — 2Corinthians 1:5

Come. Follow Him. Look forward to His return.

> *What do you see when you think about following Jesus? Glory or pain?*

> *Are you ever tempted to stop short in your following because of potential suffering?*

> *Jesus, bless me with the vision to look forward with thanks and praise.*

Father God, as You teach me Your Word, help me to see who You are and praise You openly. (Psalm 119:171)

December 21
4 Days til Christmas

Stirred Up

Matthew 2:1-6

Jesus — the image of the invisible God, firstborn over all creation, for whom and by whom all things were made (Colossians 1:15-16) — entered the world as a baby, creating a stir in the heavens and on earth.

A brilliant star appeared capturing the attention of wise men — the Magi — who packed up and moved out on an elaborate road trip to worship the newborn king of the Jews. In their wisdom, they headed straight for Jerusalem, the center of Jewish worship and culture. Their search alerted King Herod and all those in positions of authority who reacted with fear. Various translations of the Bible use: *disturbed, troubled, terrified.* Hearts were stirred.

Two groups of people, two different reactions. The Magi, though not Jewish, looked outside themselves seeking truth and the things of God. The Jewish rulers, wrapped up in the world, focused on their own interests;

the maintenance of power and influence, their primary concern. Seekers rejoiced over the birth of Jesus, going to great lengths to welcome Him into the world. The power-hungry felt threatened by the arrival of a new king and began a search to locate the One who challenged their authority.

Jesus's presence, even as an infant, stirs things up. He is Lord — Sovereign in all creation. Revelation of the King is followed by one of two responses: humble worship or fearful agitation. Unbelievers, believing they control their destinies, typically take a defensive stance, but they are not the only ones with kingdoms to protect. Believers, those who profess to know and love the King, also resist His authority. I'm continually taken by surprise when Jesus steps into my unsurrendered territory. Word of the King challenges my sense of independence and pride. My heart wrestles with humbly seeking the truth or digging in to defend my domain...

Jesus will establish His Lordship in every area of a Believer's life: finances... entertainment... relationships... schedules... We can battle with Him and resist His ways or we can come into agreement with who He is and surrender all. *Are there areas in your life where news of the King disturbs your peace? Do you respond with humble devotion or go on the defensive?* Jesus is Lord. We deceive ourselves when we refuse to submit to His authority in everything.

King of kings and Lord of lords — Jesus stirs up hearts — He always has, He always will. News of the King stirred the Magi's hearts to worship. Herod and his cohorts were just plain agitated.

...the thoughts of many hearts will be revealed...
—Luke 2:35

Who He is reveals who we are.

Do you see evidence in the world today of "the thoughts of hearts being revealed" because of the celebration of Jesus' birth? Explain.

What does His presence reveal about you?

———————————————

Lord, You are the King. Help me to work through the power struggles in my heart. I surrender.

———————————————

Lord, fill me with the desire and ability to do what You say. I want to live an "unshakable" life. (Luke 6:46-48)

December 22
3 Days til Christmas

The Journey

Matthew 2:7-11

God makes His presence clear to those who actively seek Him.

> *Ask and it will be given to you; seek and you will find; knock and the door will be opened to you.*
> —Matthew 7:7

The Magi sought the King of the Jews. Arriving in Jerusalem — the city of the temple of God and the Jewish people — they asked where they could find the newborn King. They received directions to Bethlehem.

> *Ask and it will be given to you...*

The Magi continued seeking, following the star until it stopped. They rejoiced!

> *...seek and you will find...*

At the house, they found Mary and Jesus. They bowed down, worshipped, and gave gifts fit for a newborn King. The Magi supplied this family of meager means with gold and expensive herbs known to have medicinal benefits for babies.

...knock and the door will be opened to you.

God promises: if you seek Him, you will find Him (Jeremiah 29:13) — *seek* being the operative word. The Magi intentionally prepared and set off on their journey. Travel was slow and difficult, their destination unclear, yet these wise men willingly took the risk. Nothing distracted them. Focused on the star, they held onto the hope of worshiping the King of the Jews.

When I chose to seek the King, I intentionally reordered my life. Prior to this decision, my focus was exercise. As a stay-at-home mom with three small children, I didn't allow myself a shower until I spent time on my stair-stepper. The day I began my journey to seek God, prayer and time in the Bible replaced exercise as a priority. My commitment: *No shower until I spent time seeking God.*

Being a new Christian, the journey seemed slow and my approach to Scripture unsure. God graciously led me to devotionals and Bible studies, giving me guidance and providing focus. Unlike the Magi, my journey has no geographical end. I'm prepared to continue seeking Him with the hope of an ever-deepening relationship. God continues to lead me to places of worship, and reveals Himself in new ways as I seek Him throughout my days.

God is faithful. If you seek Him, you will find Him. If you have doubts, all you have to do is actively search for Him. Seek His presence in creation, His fingerprints are everywhere. Seek Him in the Bible, He is the Word made flesh (John 1:14). If you really want to know the Truth, spend time and energy seeking... you will find Him. It's a promise.

> *But if from there you seek the Lord your God, you will find him if you seek him with all your heart and with all your soul.* —Deuteronomy 4:29

Join the Wise Men on their journey — seek the King with a focused intentional commitment and hope.

> *Have you intentionally set out on a journey to seek God? Why or why not?*

> *Do you take time to seek God every day? How?*

> *Heavenly Father, You desire to be found by those who desire You. I choose to seek You. Teach me to be intentional, committed, and focused on the journey.*

Father, direct my footsteps as I read Your Word;
let no sin rule over me. (Psalm 119:133)

December 23
2 Days til Christmas

Faithfulness

Matthew 2:12-18

God is faithful to the faithful, to His Word, to His purpose, to His character.

> *To the faithful you show yourself faithful... but*
> *to the devious you show yourself shrewd.* — Psalm
> 18:25-26

The Magi faithfully followed the star, a part of God's plan to provide for and protect His Son. He warned them in a dream not to return to Herod. God is faithful to those who are faithful.

Another faithful follower, another dream, Joseph responded to the warning without hesitation. God protected His Son against the fury of a murderous king. Matthew reveals the connection to Scripture, an escape and a slaughter. God is faithful to His Word.

King Herod, faithful only to himself, proved to be devious. God shrewdly frustrated his plan. No man or nation can interfere with God's plans (Psalm 33:10-11). Jesus would fulfill the purpose for which He was sent. God is faithful to His purpose.

Faithful? Protecting one, at the cost of many... a fulfillment of prophecy? What about sacrificing the one crazed king instead of an untold number of babies? Presented here is a scenario that challenges the faith of the faithful. Every day, similar events take place in the world, circumstantial evidence against a Sovereign God who claims to be good. Can you trust God to be good when bad things happen to the seemingly innocent? Is there room in your faith for a God who redeems disastrous outcomes in this world, transforming them into eternal blessing and joy?

The faithful faithfully trust God to be who He says He is. From the world's perspective, the crucifixion of the Son of God looked like an unmitigated disaster. Yet the spiritual reality of the cross was — and *is* — the greatest demonstration of God's love and power (Ephesians 2:4-5). God is faithful to His character.

In my own experience, I have found Him to be nothing but faithful... by faith I say this, for my flesh wants to say: *Really?* My flesh sees times of failure... feels the pain of rejection... Stepping out in faith, delivering a word, dismissed in short order, whisked out a door. After pushing the envelope of your faith and comfort zone, rejection can make you question the trustworthiness of God.

The faithful consider God trustworthy. They are *trust-full*. Trusting His knowledge of their motive... even if they misunderstand the call. Trusting Him with whatever the outcome... God has a plan and purpose in it. Even in pain... they choose to trust. God is God. He is good. He cannot lie. He is faithful.

Throughout Jesus' life, God confused and frustrated those bent on destroying His Son — those faithful only to themselves. God faithfully protects and guides the ones who desire to fulfill His purpose. With or without you, God's plans never fail. His purpose is always fulfilled. He is faithful.

Are you faithful to God or frustrated by God? Explain.

Do you currently have the faith to trust God in the midst of "senseless" suffering? Are you willing to try?

_____

Forgive me, Lord, when I doubt Your faithfulness. You are trustworthy. Bless me with faith in Your Word, Your purpose, and Your character.

_____

Lord, Your Word is living and active, help me to see its effects in my life. Reveal the thoughts and attitudes of my heart in need of change. (Hebrews 4:12)

December 24
1 Day til Christmas

A Walk in the Dark
Matthew 2:19-23

For the third time, Joseph received direction through a dream. Each time he had a choice: obey or disobey.

Throughout this story, God gave Joseph specific and difficult guidance: *Do not abandon Mary and her baby, take her home as your wife... Pack up your family in the middle of the night and go to a place you've never been for an indefinite period of time...* Obedience was not the only option — Joseph could have made different choices.

Why put up with the social stigma of an "adulterous" wife? Why sneak out of town to a foreign country for who knows how long? Kings aren't threatened by babies. And now, another move... is it really necessary? From a worldly perspective, God's directions seem radical and illogical. However, Joseph chose to rely on God's eternal perspective.

> *Who among you fears the Lord and obeys the word of his servant? Let the one who walks in the dark, who has no light, trust in the name of the Lord and rely on their God.* —Isaiah 50:10

Joseph recognized his limitations, he *walked in the dark*. He trusted God and obediently packed up his family for the move.

Obedience to God's call often feels like walking in the dark. Several years ago, I hesitated on my way to visit my mother-in-law in the hospital, I was empty-handed... no flowers, no balloon, not even a card. I considered picking up lunch... except, God interrupted my thoughts with His plan as I sat at a red-light...

Holy Spirit: *Just go to the hospital.*

Me: *But I don't have anything to take.* (As if He didn't know!)

Holy Spirit: *Just go.*

By the time the light turned green, I thought... *OK, I'll just go. But I feel bad not taking anything.*

To my surprise, when I arrived they were in the process of being discharged. My in-laws needed one thing, a ride home! I boldly announced that God had sent me to give them a ride. I was not empty-handed... I just didn't know it. Thanksgiving sang in my heart the rest of the day — God made me a blessing. I also realized that I almost missed the opportunity... God continually amazes me, yet still, I struggle with obedience. It's hard to walk in the dark...

Joseph's testimony of bold obedience sets a high standard for us to follow. For those of us who struggle more than Joseph, God provides three informers to guide us in making decisions both large and small: the Bible, the Holy Spirit, and the fellowship of Believers. The more familiar we become with the informers, the more we will hear them and trust them. The direction they give may not be the easiest option or make much sense at the time, but it will be the right one. Trust God. Choose to obey.

When you make decisions do you consult the informers: Bible, Holy Spirit and Believers?

Are you tempted to take the easy road when you know the more difficult road is the right one? Explain.

Help me recognize the limits of my knowledge, Lord. You know everything and see everything — please direct me through Your Word, Your Spirit, and Your Church. Give me the boldness to trust and obey.

Heavenly Father, as I read Your Word, reveal its truth and timeless nature to my heart. (Psalm 119:160)

December 25
Christmas

The Greatest Gift

John 3:16

At the heart of Bethlehem lies Jesus…
God's one and only Son...
A gift of grace to the world...

On our journey we've seen that God created the world for people and people for Himself. His sole desire, a close loving relationship.

We've seen His creation reject Him and choose a lie instead of the truth, disobedience breaking the relationship. We made ourselves God's enemies (Romans 5:10, Colossians 1:21).

We've seen God's love, mercy, and compassion make a way for us to return. The price of sin is death. A price Jesus chose to pay on our behalf. The only One who was without sin, the only One undeserving of death...

*...whoever **believes in** him shall not perish but have eternal life...*

Believe in — two words — the key to life everlasting. What do they mean? How do we unwrap the gift? The Greek word translated as *believe* means more than just accepting in the mind, it means to have faith in, trust (Dictionary of Biblical Languages). Your life reveals what you truly believe. We act on what we trust. If you believe in Jesus, you follow His way and obey His commands. The small word translated as *in* conveys the idea of motion, going deeper into any place or thing (Greek-English Lexicon). To *believe in*, as the Scripture says, is to *obediently trust Jesus more and more...* then you shall not perish but have eternal life!

An ongoing, trusting, growing relationship with Jesus is a picture of *believe in* — a relationship ensuring freedom from sin and death, freedom to find and fulfill your purpose in life, freedom to build a friendship with your Creator. This is the gift of Christmas and the reason we respond by graciously giving gifts to others.

Before you give or receive another gift, consider if you have unwrapped the Greatest Gift. If you would like to receive this gift now, all you have to do is tell God. With a sincere trusting heart and a short prayer tell Him you believe...

Heavenly Father, I trust Jesus is Your Son and that He died for my sins. I am a sinner and I desperately need the gift of salvation He offers. Jesus, I give You my life. Forgive me and lead me in a relationship with You. Thank You for loving me to death. Amen.

If you received the Greatest Gift, let someone know. If you have more questions, seek and you will find. The gift is waiting to be received.

Merry Christmas!

Bibliography

Dictionary of Biblical Languages:

Swanson, James. *Dictionary of Biblical Languages With Semantic Domains: Greek (New Testament).* electronic ed. Oak Harbor: Logos Research Systems, Inc., 1997.

Enhanced Strong's Lexicon:

Strong, James. *Enhanced Strong's Lexicon.* Bellingham, WA: Logos Bible Software, 2001.

Greek-English Lexicon:

Louw, Johannes P. and Eugene Albert Nida. *Greek-English Lexicon of the New Testament: Based on Semantic Domains.* electronic ed. of the 2nd edition. New York: United Bible Societies, 1996.

Webster's:

Merriam-Webster, Inc. *Merriam-Webster's Collegiate Dictionary.* Eleventh ed. Springfield, MA: Merriam-Webster, Inc., 2003.

About the Author

Carol B. Weaver is an ordinary Christian, filled with a passion for God and His Word. She has led Sunday School classes, Bible studies, and multiple prayer groups during her 23 year walk with Christ. The journaling of thoughts and revelations led to a call to share the truth of God's Word with others through devotionals. Carol has been published in The Upper Room Magazine and currently blogs at JeremiahsMenu.blog and SisterTalkFaith.com. She lives with her husband in the piney woods of East Texas. She also co-owns a downtown shop where she and her business partner write Bible studies and teach for their ministry, Sister Talk: Faith.

Printed in the United States
By Bookmasters